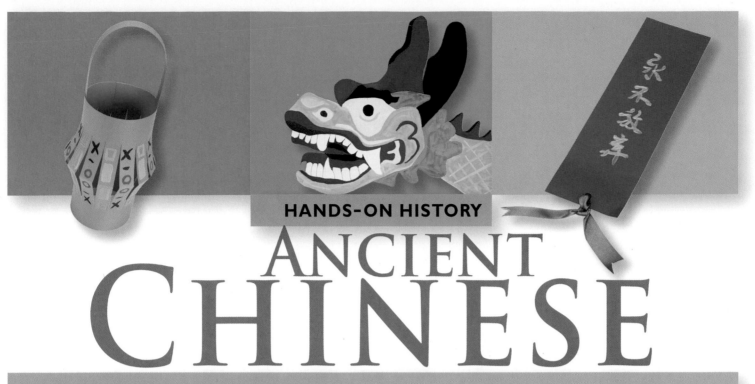

HANDS-ON HISTORY

ANCIENT
CHINESE

DRESS, EAT, WRITE, AND PLAY JUST LIKE THE CHINESE

JOE FULLMAN

QEB Publishing

Library of Congress Cataloging-in-Publication Data

Fullman, Joe.
  Ancient Chinese : dress, eat, and play just like the ancient Chinese
/ Joe Fullman.
    p. cm. -- (QEB hands-on history)
  Includes index.
  ISBN 978-1-59566-243-9 (hardcover)
  1. China--Civilization--221 B.C.-960 A.D.--Juvenile literature. I.
Title.
  DS747.37.F85 2010
  931--dc22

                                    2009001113

Printed and bound in China

Author Joe Fullman
Consultant John Malam
Editor Ben Hubbard
Designer Lisa Peacock
Project Maker Veronica Lenz

Publisher Steve Evans
Creative Director Zeta Davies
Managing Editor Amanda Askew

Picture credits
(t=top, b=bottom, l=left, r=right, c=center, fc=front cover)

Alamy Images 12b Lou Linwei, 14c Eddie Gerald/DK,
18b Dennis Cox, 28bl dbimages/Allen Brown
Bridgeman Art Library 16t Free Library/Philadelphia,
PA, USA, 17t Free Library, Philadelphia, PA, USA/Girau-
don, 18tr Musee Guimet, Paris, France/Bonora Giraudon
Corbis 6b Robert Harding World Imagery , 8bl Zeng
Nian, 8t Christie's Images, 14b Jim Sugar, 16bl Liu Liqun,
18tl Christie's Images, 23tl Liu Liqun, 29t Rob Howard
Getty Images 4c The Bridgeman Art Library, 9t The
Bridgeman Art Library, 12t The Bridgeman Art Library,
20t The Bridgeman Art Library, 28t The Image Bank/
Steve Allen
Photolibrary 14t Richard T Nowitz, 22b Vidler Vidler,
22t North Wind Picture Archives
Rex Features 26br
Shutterstock 4b Michael Rubin, 6t Pichugin Dmitry, 7tl
JCElv, 10b Ke Wang, 10t Sunxuejun, 24b Craig Hanson,
26bl design56, 26t John Leung
Simon Pask 5tl, 5tr, 5cl, 5cr, 5bl, 5br, 7tc, 7tr, 7cl, 7cr, 7bl,
7br, 8c, 8br, 9cl, 9cr, 9bl, 9br, 11tl, 11tr, 11cl, 11cr 11bl, 11br,
13tr, 13cl, 13cr, 13bl, 13br, 15tl, 15tr, 15cl, 15cr, 15b, 16cr,
16br, 17cl, 17cr, 17bl,17br, 19tl, 19tr, 19cr, 19bl, 19br, 21tl,
21tr, 21cl, 21 cr, 21bl, 21br, 23tr, 23cl, 23cr, 23bl, 23br, 25tr,
25cl, 25cr, 25bl, 25br, 27tl, 27tr, 27cl, 27cr, 27bl, 27br, 28cr,
28br, 29cl, 29cr, 29bl, 29br
Topham Picturepoint 13tl The Board of Trustees of the
Armouries/HIP, 20b The Granger Collection, 24t Museum
of East Asian Art/HIP

**TAKE CARE
WHEN USING SCISSORS**

Words in **bold** are
explained in the glossary
on page 30.

Website information is correct at the time
of going to press. However, the publishers
cannot accept liability for any information
or links found on third-party websites.

Before undertaking an activity that involves
eating or the preparation of food, parents
and/or teachers should ensure that none
of the children in their care are allergic
to any of the ingredients. In a classroom
situation, prior written permission from
parents may be required.

CONTENTS

WHO WERE THE ANCIENT CHINESE?

The ancient Chinese were a people who lived in a country we now call China. China was **founded** in 221 BC. Before then, the people lived in a number of separate **states**. Each state was ruled by a lord. These states were often at war. Eventually, one state defeated all the others and brought the country together. It was ruled by a family known as the Qin (or Ch'in), which is where the word China comes from. The lord of the Qin became the first emperor of China.

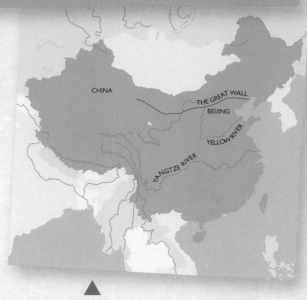

China is a large country in Asia.

LONG SUCCESS

The Chinese Empire lasted for more than 2,000 years. In that time, the country was ruled by a series of powerful families, who fought each other for control of the country. The emperor was the head of the family. When a family ruled for more than one **generation**, it became known as a dynasty. These dynasties often fought each other for control of the country. In 1912, the Chinese people became a **democracy** and got rid of the last dynasty.

GREAT INVENTORS

During the time of the dynasties, the people of China came up with many inventions that are still used today, including paper, kites, and umbrellas. Ancient China also produced many great thinkers and artists who have become famous throughout the world.

Chinese emperors were powerful people who were carried from place to place in carriages by teams of servants.

Dragon boats are very colorful. They are powered by rowers who row to the rhythm of a drum.

DID YOU KNOW?

EACH CHINESE YEAR IS NAMED AFTER ONE OF 12 SIGNS OF THE CHINESE ZODIAC. THESE ARE THE RAT, OX, TIGER, CAT, DRAGON, SNAKE, HORSE, GOAT, MONKEY, ROOSTER, DOG, AND PIG.

MAKE A DRAGON BOAT HEAD

In China, dragons are seen as helpful creatures. Since ancient times, people have raced dragon boats with a model dragon head at the front.

YOU WILL NEED
TRACING PAPER • CARDSTOCK
PENCIL • RULER • SCISSORS
PAINTBRUSH AND PAINTS • PEN

1

Cut out a square of tracing paper and divide it into a grid of five squares by five squares.

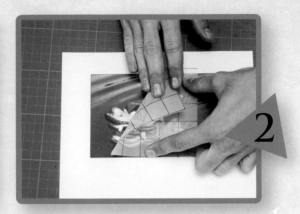

2

Place the tracing paper over the picture of the dragon's head below. Trace the head onto the paper.

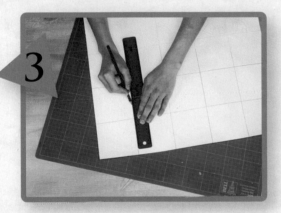

3

Cut out a large square of cardstock and divide it into a grid of five squares by five squares.

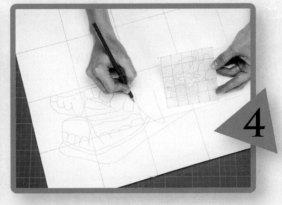

4

Copy the pictures on the tracing paper squares into the larger squares on the cardstock.

5

Use paints to color in the dragon you have made. When dry, cut out your dragon head.

The Chinese believe ▶ that the dragon is a symbol of good luck.

5

MOUNTAINS, DESERTS, AND RIVERS

The world's tallest mountains, the Himalayas, border China to the west.

China is a very big country. In the west are giant mountains called the Himalayas. In the north is the dry, dusty Gobi Desert. In the east are flat **plains** where two of world's longest rivers flow the Yangtze River and the Yellow River. Most ancient Chinese towns were built in the east. Here, the land was flat enough to build houses on.

WATERY ROADS

Waterways were a very important part of ancient Chinese **civilization**. Many towns were built on **canals** where people would use boats to get around. In the 6th century AD, a giant waterway, known as the Grand Canal, was built to join the country's two main rivers. It was used to transport rice, China's main **crop**, from the south to the north. The canal is 1,100 miles (1770 kilometers) long and is still used today.

Boats have been transporting goods up and down China's Grand Canal for more than a thousand years.

ALL ALONE

For many thousands of years, the Chinese thought they were the only people in the world. The great mountains and wide deserts surrounding the country made it very difficult for anyone to get in or out. It was only in the 2nd century BC that the Chinese met people from the outside world and realized that there were other civilizations.

Make a 3D Map of China

China is a vast country of towering mountains, barren deserts, wild rivers, and fast-growing cities.

This map shows China's mountains, deserts, rivers, and Great Wall.

YOU WILL NEED
NEWSPAPER • LARGE GREEN CARDSTOCK • PEN • GLUE PAINTBRUSH AND PAINTS BLUE YARN • SAND BROWN SUGAR CUBES SCISSORS

1

Using the map at the top of the page, copy a larger version onto green cardstock.

2

The dark area shows mountains. Scrunch up small pieces of newspaper and glue to the cardstock. Paint brown.

3

The lines across the middle show rivers. Braid three pieces of blue yarn together and glue to the cardstock.

4

The light areas show deserts. Cover the area on your cardstock with glue and sprinkle sand on top.

Carefully cut out your 3D map of China.
▼

5

The brown line across the middle is the Great Wall of China. Glue sugar cubes to the paper and paint brown.

7

GODS AND RELIGION

The ancient Chinese worshipped many different gods. They believed these gods controlled everything in the world. They also believed that their relatives became gods when they died, so they worshipped them, too. During the time of the dynasties, people in China followed three main religions—**Taoism**, **Confucianism**, and **Buddhism**. All three religions told people to live peaceful lives and not to go to war or harm other people.

◀ This bronze statue is of Buddha, the founder of Buddhism, who was born in 563 BC.

PUT ON A SHADOW PUPPET PLAY

The ancient Chinese used lights and puppets to put on shadow plays, which told stories about gods and heroes.

Traditional Chinese shadow puppet shows are still performed throughout the country.

▼

YOU WILL NEED
WHITE SHEET • PENCIL
SCISSORS • 4 WOODEN STICKS
CARDSTOCK • FLASHLIGHT
STICKY TAPE • PAINTBRUSH
AND PAINTS

1

Copy the puppets on page 9. The people should be 6 in (15 cm) high and the dragon 10 in (25 cm) long.

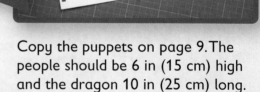

2

Cut out the puppets and paint them black. When dry, tape the wooden sticks to the backs.

8

THREE RELIGIONS

Taoists believe that all living things contain a special force that people should respect. Confucianists follow the teachings of Confucius. He thought people should follow their leaders and gods. Buddhists believe that everyone can lead happier lives if they give up their possessions.

DID YOU KNOW?
THE FIRST PEOPLE ARRIVED IN THE LAND WE NOW CALL CHINA AROUND 50,000 YEARS AGO.

ORACLE BONES

The ancient Chinese used animal bones, called Oracle Bones, to try to predict the future. A priest would write a question on an animal bone. The bones would then be heated until they cracked. The cracks would form patterns, which the priest could read to answer the question.

Confucius was a great philosopher in the 5th century BC.

3 Hang up the white sheet. The audience should be on one side, the puppets and the flashlight on the other.

You could use paper fasteners and extra wooden sticks to make your puppets' legs and arms move.

4 Shine the flashlight at the sheet. Use the sticks to hold the puppets up to the sheet and perform a play.

THE EMPEROR

The emperor was the most powerful person in China. The Chinese people called him the "Son of Heaven," and believed he was a god. Everyone below the emperor had to do what the emperor said. Emperors lived in huge palaces, looked after by thousands of servants. They were also guarded by large armies. Most emperors were the sons of emperors.

▲ Once closed to visitors, the Forbidden City is today a popular tourist attraction.

THE GREAT WALL OF CHINA

In the 3rd century BC, Qin Shi Huang, the first emperor of China, ordered his people to build an enormous wall. It was meant to protect China against attacks by northern tribes. It is the longest wall ever built and still stands today, stretching for 4,160 miles (6,700 kilometers) across northern China.

DID YOU KNOW?

FROM THE 14TH CENTURY AD TO THE EARLY 20TH CENTURY, EMPERORS LIVED IN BEIJING, THE COUNTRY'S CAPITAL, IN THE LARGEST PALACE IN THE WORLD. IT WAS CALLED THE FORBIDDEN CITY BECAUSE NO ONE WAS ALLOWED TO ENTER WITHOUT THE EMPEROR'S PERMISSION.

ARMY OF THE DEAD

The first emperor of China was buried along with more than 8,000 life-size clay soldiers, known today as the Terracotta Army. Each clay soldier held a real bronze weapon to defend the emperor in the afterlife. There were also clay chariots and horses, as well as musicians and acrobats. Buried in 210 BC, the soldiers were only rediscovered in AD 1974, more than 2,000 years later.

◀ Thousands of workers were employed to build the emperor's tomb and the Terracotta Army.

MAKE A TERRACOTTA SOLDIER

In the Terracotta Army all the soldiers are different. Each statue has its own clothing, hairstyle, and facial expression.

YOU WILL NEED
MODELING CLAY
MODELING TOOLS

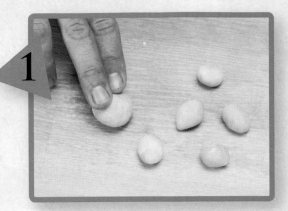

1

Roll out a ball of clay for the body and five smaller balls for the arms, legs, and head.

2

Mold the shape of the body. Take another piece of clay and mold the skirt. Stick the skirt on the body.

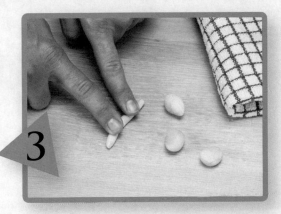

3

Roll two balls into sausage shapes for the legs and feet. Repeat for the arms and hands.

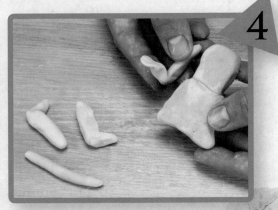

4

Attach the head, arms, and legs to the body. Mold hands and feet at the end of the arms and legs.

5

Make a thin roll of clay and attach as a collar. Use a modeling tool to draw on the face, hair, and armor.

You could make several soldiers and form your own Terracotta Army.

11

NOBLES AND ARTISANS

Traditional Chinese homes had overhanging roofs that were believed to protect the houses against evil spirits.

The emperor and his family were the most important people in ancient China. The next most important people were the **nobles**. They owned most of the country's land and grew very wealthy by collecting **taxes** from the people who lived there. The nobles used their money to buy large houses and expensive clothes, weapons, and jewelry.

DID YOU KNOW?
SOME ANCIENT CHINESE CITIES WERE VERY LARGE. BOTH XI'AN AND LIN-AN HAD POPULATIONS OF MORE THAN A MILLION PEOPLE.

CITIES
Most nobles lived in cities. The Chinese were one of the first people to build and live in large cities. Rich people, such as nobles, usually lived at one end of the city, while poor people lived at the other end. Each city was surrounded by a high wall. Every night, the gates in the wall would be locked, stopping anyone from getting in or out.

The great walls of Pingyao city were built in the 14th century. They are 40 feet (12 meters) high, 19.700 feet (6,000 meters) long and have 72 watchtowers.

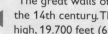

OTHER CLASSES

After the nobles, the next most important people in ancient China were the **artisans**. These were the people who made things, such as weapons, jewelry, and silk. China also had many merchants, who traded goods with people both in China and in other lands.

Make swords with different decorations on the handle. Then you can pretend to battle with your friends. ▶

◀ This type of sword was known as a dao in ancient China. The sword had one sharp edge and was slightly curved.

YOU WILL NEED
THICK CARDSTOCK • PENCIL
ALUMINUM FOIL • SCISSORS
PAINTBRUSH AND METALLIC
PAINT • STRING BEADS • RULER
MARKER PEN • HOLE PUNCH

MAKE A CHINESE SWORD

Chinese nobles had to fight in the emperor's army. They could afford to buy the best swords, which would be decorated with patterns.

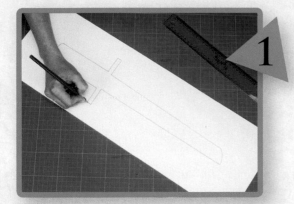

Draw a sword shape onto cardstock. The blade should be 12 in (30 cm) long, the handle 4 in (10 cm) long.

Cut it out and paint the handle with metallic paint. When dry, draw the decoration onto the handle.

Cut a piece of foil longer than the blade and twice as wide. Wrap the foil tightly around the blade.

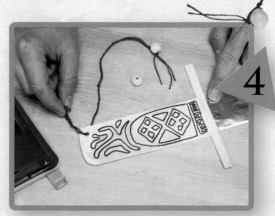

Make a hole in the end of the handle. Thread the piece of string through the hole, add the beads, and tie in a knot.

WAR AND WARRIORS

The Chinese people often went to war with each other. Before China became one country, the separate parts, or states, fought many battles. This time was known as the Warring States period. When China became one, the emperor still had to fight against enemies who tried to steal his throne. War happened so often in China that a general called Sun Tzu even wrote an entire book about fighting. It is called the *The Art of War*.

▶ This helmet and suit of armor were found buried in the tomb of an emperor from the Ming dynasty (1368–1644 BC).

WEAPONS

The Chinese fought using axes and **Jis** made of bronze. Nobles would ride into battle on chariots pulled by horses. Ordinary soldiers fought on foot. Battles in China usually began with armies firing arrows at each other using **crossbows**. Crossbows were invented in China in the 5th century BC. These weapons could fire **bolts** very fast and far.

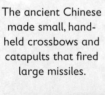

▲ The ancient Chinese made small, hand-held crossbows and catapults that fired large missiles.

DID YOU KNOW?
SOME CHINESE WARRIORS WORE ARMOR MADE OF SMALL IRON PLATES. IT WAS SO HEAVY THAT SOLDIERS WOULD SOMETIMES TAKE IT OFF SO THEY COULD SWING THEIR WEAPONS MORE EASILY.

WAR GAMES

Some scholars believe that ancient Chinese army leaders practiced their war plans by playing board games, such as Go (also known as Wéiqi). Go has been played in China for more than 3,000 years.

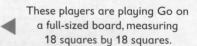

◀ These players are playing Go on a full-sized board, measuring 18 squares by 18 squares.

MAKE A GO BOARD

To win at Go you must capture more areas of the board than your opponent—just like an army tries to capture more areas of land to win a war.

YOU WILL NEED
CARDSTOCK • PEN • RULER
24 RED BEADS • 24 BLUE BEADS

1

Divide a square of cardstock into a grid, eight squares by eight squares.

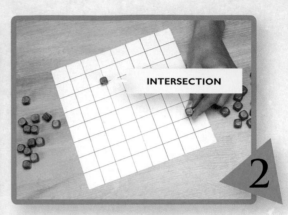

2

INTERSECTION

Take turns placing your pieces on any intersection (the place where two lines cross). Blue goes first.

3

GROUP

GROUP

Form groups by placing your pieces next to each other horizontally or vertically (but not diagonally).

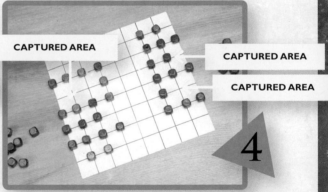

CAPTURED AREA

CAPTURED AREA

CAPTURED AREA

4

Surround, or "capture," an area of the board before your opponent has a chance to put their pieces there.

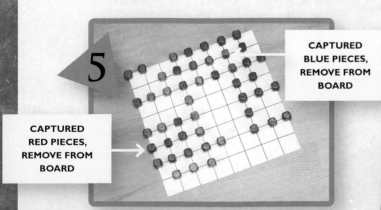

5

CAPTURED BLUE PIECES, REMOVE FROM BOARD

CAPTURED RED PIECES, REMOVE FROM BOARD

You can also capture an opponent's piece, or pieces, by surrounding it with your pieces. Remove their pieces.

WHO WINS?

RULES FOR TWO PLAYERS

Take turns putting pieces on the board until there are no pieces left. Then count up how many intersections lie within your captured areas. These include intersections on the edge of the board. You get one point per intersection and a point for every one of your opponent's pieces you have captured. Whoever has the most points wins.

FARMERS AND PEASANTS

Most of the people in ancient China were not rich and did not live in cities. They were peasants and worked in the fields, looking after the crops and animals. Most peasants did not own the land they farmed. It belonged to the nobles. The peasants would have to give some of the food they grew to the nobles. They would also have to help build the nobles' houses.

Ancient Chinese peasants harvesting rice from a flooded **paddy field**. ▶

MAKE A STRAW HAT

Hats made of straw were worn by peasants working in the fields. The wide brims protected their faces against the sun and rain.

YOU WILL NEED
YELLOW CARDSTOCK • PLATE
PENCIL • SCISSORS • GLUE
RIBBON • RULER • STICKY TAPE

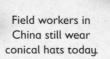

◀ Field workers in China still wear conical hats today.

1

Take a large plate, place it on the cardstock and draw around it. Carefully cut out the circle.

4

Fold the non-glued side over the glued side to form a cone.

HARD LIFE

Life on a farm was hard. All the family would work together in the fields. Most jobs were done by hand. The peasants would plow the earth, plant the seeds, and carry the crops and water themselves. Only rich farmers could afford to use animals to pull **plows** or carry things.

◀ Farm workers often used an ox to pull their cart through a paddy field.

HOUSES AND MACHINES

In summer, peasants slept in cool huts with thin bamboo walls. In winter, they moved to warmer houses with thick mud walls. The Chinese invented many machines that helped make farming easier. These included machines for **irrigating** the fields.

DID YOU KNOW?
IN 207 BC, THE PEASANTS IN CHINA FELT THEY WERE BEING TREATED BADLY BY THEIR RULERS—SO THEY REBELLED AND OVERTHREW THE EMPEROR.

2
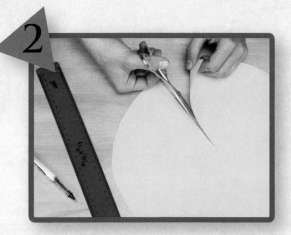

Mark the center of the circle. Draw a line from the center to the edge. Cut along this line.

3

Glue along one edge of the line.

5
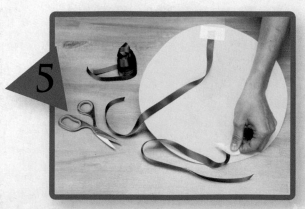

Stick one end of each ribbon inside the hat, one on either side. Tie the ribbons under your chin.

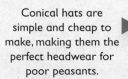
Conical hats are simple and cheap to make, making them the perfect headwear for poor peasants. ▶

17

CLOTHES AND MAKE-UP

Rich and poor people wore very different clothes in ancient China. Noble men and women wore expensive robes, **tunics**, trousers, and slippers. These were dyed bright colors with **pigment** made from plants. They were also decorated with pictures of animals and plants. Poor people wore simple, uncolored clothes, often made from a rough, coarse fabric called ramie. They also wore straw sandals.

Some merchants in ancient China became very rich. This merchant's wife is wearing an expensive silk robe.

A bronze hair comb from the 7th century AD.

HAIR AND MAKE-UP

Both men and women had long hair. Men wore their hair on top of their head in a **topknot**. Women arranged their hair in special styles using pins and combs and kept themselves cool with delicate fans. Women put make-up on their faces. Rich men and women wore jewelry made of gold and **jade**, which the Chinese thought was the most precious of all materials.

DID YOU KNOW?
WOMEN IN ANCIENT CHINA CHANGED THE SHAPE OF THEIR EYEBROWS TO FOLLOW FASHION. SOMETIMES THEY PAINTED THEM IN A CURVE. SOMETIMES THEY PAINTED THEM IN AN UPSIDE DOWN "V" SHAPE.

Fans are still very popular in China. These people are practicing using their fans.

SILK

The best clothes were made of a special cloth called silk. Silk is made by weaving threads taken from the **cocoons** of the mulberry moth. The larvae that make these cocoons are called silk worms. Silk worms were very valuable in ancient China and cost a lot of money.

MAKE A CHINESE FAN

Both men and women in ancient China used hand fans to stay cool on a hot summer day.

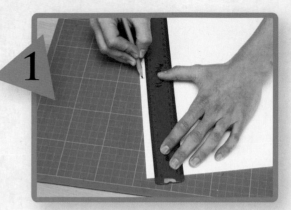

1

Measure out a strip of paper 30 in (76 cm) by 6 in (15 cm). Cut out.

2

Paint a picture on the paper, such as a dragon.

3

Glue the wooden sticks to either end of the paper. Fold the paper into pleats, each 1 in (2 cm) wide, like a concertina.

Wave the fan in front of your face to cool down.

4

To open the fan, push the two wooden sticks together, until the fan becomes a circle.

CLEVER INVENTIONS

The ancient Chinese came up with many inventions that changed the world. The emperors asked scientists to invent machines that would improve the life of the Chinese people. Many Chinese inventions are still used today, including the bell, the compass, drums, fireworks, gunpowder, kites, paper, paper money, printing, playing cards, silk, the toothbrush, and the umbrella.

DID YOU KNOW?
THE CHINESE INVENTED A TYPE OF MEDICINE CALLED ACUPUNCTURE. THIS INVOLVES STICKING THIN NEEDLES INTO A PATIENT'S BODY TO RELIEVE PAIN.

BIG BANGS
Gunpowder was invented in China in the 8th century AD. It is a powder that explodes when set alight. Gunpowder helped the Chinese to invent new weapons, such as bombs and guns, which were much more powerful than anything they had used before. The Chinese also used gunpowder to make fireworks.

◀ This 19th century painting shows Chinese people celebrating with fireworks and kites.

Made in the 9th century BC, this is the world's earliest dated printed book. ▼

PAPER AND PRINTING
Paper was one of the most important Chinese inventions. It was invented in the 2nd century AD and was made of silk. Today, paper is made from wood. In the 9th century AD, the Chinese also invented printing. This made it much easier and cheaper to produce books, which helped many people learn how to read and write.

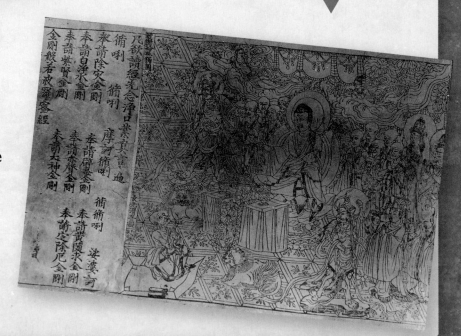

MAKE SOME PAPER

The ancient Chinese discovered they could use many different materials to make paper, including tree bark, bamboo, and even old rags.

YOU WILL NEED
WIRE COATHANGER
PANTYHOSE • BOWL • FOOD COLORING • BLENDER
NEWSPAPER PIECES • PEN
RUBBER GLOVES

1

Get an adult to twist an old wire coathanger into a square frame shape, as shown above.

2

Cut off one of the legs of the pantyhose and stretch it over the frame.

3

Fill the bowl with warm water and newspaper. Ask an adult to blend this mixture until it forms a sludge.

4

Wearing rubber gloves, add food coloring to the mixture. Pour the mixture evenly onto the frame.

5

Leave it to dry. You will soon have a new piece of colored paper.

Use your paper to write notes or letters.

TRADE AND COMMERCE

In ancient times, Chinese merchants traded, or sold, goods with many other countries and empires. In the days before planes, trains, and cars, it could take months for merchants to reach faraway countries. Merchants rode teams of camels, called caravans, which were loaded with the country's most precious goods, including teas, spices, porcelain, and silk. These caravans travelled to India, Asia, and Europe along a long route called the Silk Road.

◄ A trade caravan makes its way along the Silk Road. Merchants brought silk to Europe and gold back to China along this route.

Junks were invented during the Han Dynasty between 220 BC and AD 200. ▼

SEA TRADE
China also traded its goods by sea. They were carried in large boats called junks. Junks were also used by members of the government to visit foreign governments and by explorers to visit new lands. Compasses were used to **navigate** the seas.

DID YOU KNOW?
The Chinese built the world's first mechanical clock in the 11th century. It stood 33 feet (10 meters) high and was powered by giant buckets of water.

MONEY
In ancient times, people often used **cowrie** shells as a form of money. The first metal coins were used in China in around 1800 BC. They were made of bronze and had holes in the middle. In the 11th century AD, China produced the world's first paper money.

MAKE A COMPASS

The Chinese invented the compass, which was used by sailors to tell what direction their boats were traveling in.

◄ Early Chinese compasses were made from lodestone, a magnetic iron ore that points north.

By the 7th century AD, the Chinese were making compasses using magnetic needles floating in water. ►

1

BLUNT END

Rub the magnet along the needle from the blunt end to the sharp end a few times.

2

Ask an adult to cut a small circle from the cork.

3

Stick the needle on top of the cork using sticky tape.

4

Place the cork in the bowl of water. The magnetized needle will point north towards the North Pole.

23

ANCIENT ART

Ancient Chinese artisans and artists were highly skilled. They made jewelry and decorative objects from many different materials, including bronze, clay, gold, jade, and ivory. The homes of nobles would be filled with these beautiful items. Chinese arts and crafts were also very popular in Europe, where they were bought and sold for large sums of money. To sell more items abroad, the emperors built large factories where artisans could work producing objects.

DID YOU KNOW?
BECAUSE PORCELAIN ORIGINATED IN CHINA, IN MANY COUNTRIES, PORCELAIN OBJECTS ARE ALSO KNOWN AS "CHINA."

PORCELAIN

China was well known for objects made from porcelain, made from a type of white clay. Plates, cups, and vases were especially popular, both with people in China and in Europe. These objects were often decorated with scenes from nature, such as trees, rivers, and mountains.

◄ Chinese pottery, such as this blue and white bowl, became popular in Europe in the 17th century.

Chinese calligraphy is the art of painting letters using a brush and ink.
▼

THE THREE PERFECTIONS

Chinese scholars, or highly educated people, were supposed to learn three art forms. These were calligraphy, poetry, and painting and they were known as the Three Perfections. To show how well skilled they were in all three, a scholar would often paint a picture and then write a poem next to it using beautiful calligraphy letters.

WRITE A CALLIGRAPHY PROVERB

The ancient Chinese liked to write short, wise sayings, called proverbs, using calligraphy letters. Pick your favorite proverb and make a bookmark.

YOU WILL NEED
RED CARDSTOCK • PENCIL
PAINTBRUSH AND GOLD PAINT
HOLE PUNCH • RIBBON
RULER • SCISSORS

安貧樂道   永不放弃

◄ Use one of these proverbs to write onto your bookmark.

Place the mark inside a book to keep your place. ►

Better happy than rich   Better late than never

1 Cut out a piece of red cardstock, 8 in (20 cm) by 2 in (6 cm). Red is a lucky color in China.

2 Copy the outline of the calligraphy letters. Chinese writing is read from top to bottom, not left to right.

3 Paint the calligraphy letters using gold paint.

4 Make a hole in the bottom of the bookmark. Thread a ribbon through the hole and tie a knot.

New Year Carnival

Dragon dances are performed at Chinese New Year festivals to bring good luck.

Ancient China had many festivals. Some of these celebrated the seasons. Some honored the gods and the emperor. Others were held to remember people's ancestors. The biggest celebration was New Year, held at the beginning of spring. It lasted for 15 days. People would enjoy feasts, light colorful lanterns, and give each other presents. There would also be lots of music and dancing. The festival is still held in China today.

LUCKY COLOR

The color red is believed to be lucky in China. At New Year, people wear red clothes and give children gifts of money in red envelopes. They also set off fireworks. It is believed that the loud noises of the fireworks drive away evil spirits.

GAMES

The ancient Chinese were very fond of games. Indoors, they played dice games, card games, and board games, such as Go. Outside, they played ball games and flew colorful kites in the sky. The Chinese also liked to make music using drums, flutes, and bells.

In China, the lanterns often have riddles written on them for children to solve.

MAKE A CHINESE LANTERN

The Festival of Lanterns takes place just after New Year. At this time, colorful lanterns are lit to chase away evil spirits.

YOU WILL NEED
COLORED PAPER, 10 IN (30 CM) BY 8 IN (20 CM)
SCISSORS • PAINTBRUSH AND PAINTS • GLUE
EXTRA PAPER

Fold the paper in half lengthways.

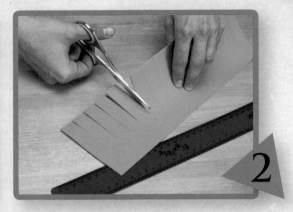

On the folded side, make 2 in (6 cm) long cuts every 1 in (2 cm), all the way along.

Unfold the paper and use the paints to decorate it.

When the paint is dry, roll the paper into a tube and glue the ends together.

To make the handle, cut a strip of paper 1 in (3 cm) by 10 in (30 cm). Curl the paper into a loop and glue the ends inside.

You could make several Chinese lanterns and hang them up in a row.

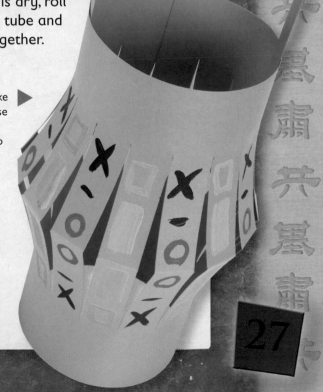

27

FOOD AND DRINK

About 7,000 years ago, the Chinese became the first people in the world to start farming rice. It soon became the country's most important crop and is still the most commonly eaten food in China today. The ancient Chinese also ate many vegetables, including soy beans. These were used to make tofu. Soy beans can also be turned into a sauce called soy sauce, which is used to flavor food.

▲ In hilly parts of China, rice is grown on flat terraces cut into the hillsides.

MAKE EGG CUSTARD DIM SUMS

Egg custard dim sums are a rich chinese delicacy.

1

YOU WILL NEED

1 EGG, BEATEN • 2 TABLESPOONS CASTER SUGAR • BAKING TRAY HALF A CUP (120 ML) MILK 8 TART CASES • JUG • MIXING BOWL • WOODEN SPOON METAL SPOON • WIRE RACK

Pour the beaten egg into the milk and add the sugar.

4

Bake the tarts in an oven for about 20 minutes at 390°F (200°C or Gas Mark 6).

▲ Dim sums are small meals, traditionally served with tea.

COOKING AND EATING

There were few forests in ancient China, so there was not much wood to make fires. To save wood, the Chinese cut their food into small pieces so that it cooked faster. Cutting food into small pieces also made it easy to pick up using **chopsticks**. Most Chinese people still use chopsticks to eat their meals today.

In modern China, food is cooked in much the same way as it was centuries ago. ▶

DRINKING

A favorite drink in ancient China was tea, which was made by putting dried leaves from the tea plant into boiling water. Tea was made in pots and then poured into small bowls, which people drank out of. The Chinese believed tea was healthy and would prevent illness.

2

Beat the mixture with the wooden spoon until it is smooth. Pour the mixture into a jug.

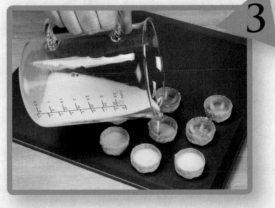

3

Pour the mixture into the tart cases, leaving a 0.5 in (1 cm) space at the top.

5

Check that they are cooked by placing a spoon end in their middle. If it comes out clean, they are done.

Custard tarts are a tasty snack. ▶

GLOSSARY

Artisan A skilled worker who makes things, usually by hand.

Bolt A short missile fired by a crossbow.

Buddhism A religion based on the teachings of Buddha, who believed people could find inner peace if they stopped worrying about their possessions.

Canal A man-made waterway, usually used for transporting goods on boats.

Chopsticks A pair of thin sticks, usually made of wood, used for eating food.

Civilization A society that shares the same culture and way of life.

Cocoon A case of silk thread spun by caterpillars, inside which they transform into moths or butterflies.

Confucianism A way of thinking based on the teachings of Confucius, who believed that people should obey the rules of families, leaders, and gods.

Cowrie A type of smooth, shiny seashell.

Crop Plants grown by people to provide food or for other uses

Crossbow A weapon that fires a missile, called a bolt.

Democracy A form of government where all the people in a country decide who should be in charge.

Founded When an area of land becomes known as a country for the first time.

Generation People who were born and live at roughly the same time.

Irrigating Watering farmland, by flowing water into fields, often through ditches or canals.

Jade A green mineral stone, which the Chinese thought had magical properties.

Ji A weapon made up of a sharp blade attached to the end of a spear.

Navigate To find out where you're going using instruments, maps, and/or the stars.

Nobles People who have been born into power by having important parents.

Paddy field A flooded field where rice is grown.

Pigment A natural substance used for dyeing or coloring things.

Plain A large, flat area of land.

Plow A farm tool used to turn over the soil and get it ready for planting crops.

State An area or country controlled by a single government or ruler.

Taoism A way of thinking based on the teachings of Lao Zi, who believed that people should live simple lives in harmony with the natural world.

Taxes Money or goods taken from people to help pay for the government.

Topknot A hairstyle in which the hair is pulled up above the head into a knot.

Tunic A loose, sleeveless item of clothing, a bit like a long waistcoat.

Waterway A river, stream, canal, or other inland body of water that can be traveled on by boat.

NOTES FOR PARENTS AND TEACHERS

- Learn about the clothes of ancient China and pick up some tips for dressing-up in a Chinese style at www.historyforkids.org/learn/china. The site also contains a wealth of information on Chinese history, philosophy, food, architecture, and many other subjects.

- Download a powerpoint presentation on the importance and significance of dragons in ancient Chinese mythology at http://presentations.pppst.com/dragons.ppt, and ask the children to make a Chinese dragon banner by using the printouts at http://scissorcraft.com/dragons5.htm.

- Learn about the traditions and history of Chinese New Year—such as cleaning the house, giving red envelopes, and lion dances—by playing a series of interactive games at http://pbskids.org/sagwa/games/index.html.

- Learn stories and tales of ancient China at http://china.mrdonn.org/stories.html, which has links to sound files, powerpoint presentations, quizzes, and websites. Get the children to create a picture book based on their favorite story.

- Look at artifacts from the museum's collection and take a series of online challenges at the British Museum's excellent ancient China site: http://www.ancientchina.co.uk/menu.html.

Useful websites

- Try your hand at online calligraphy at http://gingerbooth.com/courseware/calligraphy.html.

- Read about 4,000 years of Chinese history from the origins of Chinese civilization to the modern day at http://condensedchina.com

- If you've got a few days to spare, try making this intricate paper model of the Forbidden City: http://cp.c-ij.com/en/contents/3152/03345/index.html.